48

Understanding the Elements of the Periodic Table™

MERCURY

Kristi Lew

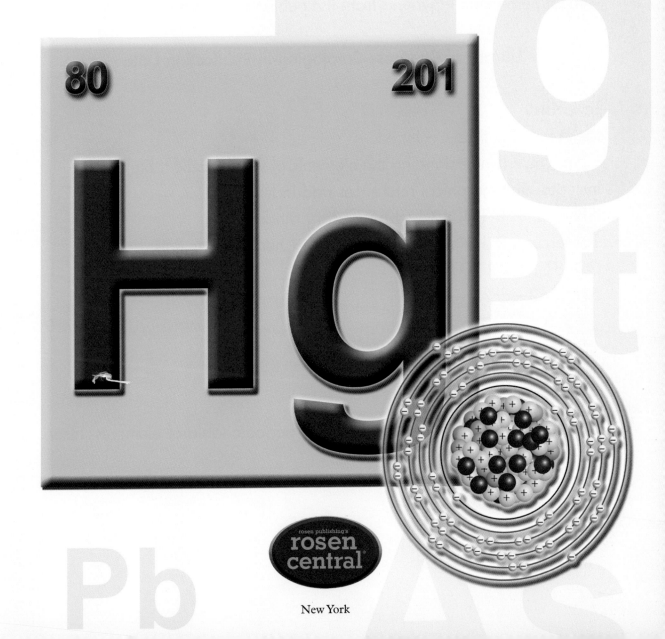

80   201

Hg

rosen publishing's
rosen
central®

New York

For our future scientists

Published in 2009 by The Rosen Publishing Group, Inc.
29 East 21st Street, New York, NY 10010

Library of Congress Cataloging-in-Publication Data

Lew, Kristi.
Mercury / Kristi Lew.—1st ed.
   p. cm.—(Understanding the elements of the periodic table)
Includes bibliographical references and index.
ISBN-13: 978-1-4042-1780-5 (library binding)
1. Mercury. 2. Periodic law—Tables. 3. Chemical elements. I. Title.
QD181.H6L49 2009
546'.663—dc22

                                                    2007044919

Manufactured in Malaysia

On the cover: Mercury's square on the periodic table of elements. Inset: The atomic structure of mercury.

Contents

Introduction

S ometimes, doctors have to be detectives, too. For example, in 1989, a family in Michigan visited their doctor when one of the sons came down with a mysterious illness. The skin on the boy's hands had turned scaly and pink. He was drooling, angered easily, and was hard to manage. After many examinations and medical tests, the boy's doctors discovered that he was suffering from pink disease. Pink disease is considered rare today, but at one time, it was a common medical problem in the United States.

The skin on the hands and feet of people who suffer from pink disease often peels off, giving these extremities a pink color. This discoloration of the hands and feet gives the disease its name. The scientific name for pink disease is acrodynia. The illness is caused when babies or young children are exposed to the element mercury (chemical symbol: Hg). In the past, mercury was an ingredient in some teething powders. These powders were used to soothe sore gums caused by emerging teeth. Unfortunately, the element mercury is also poisonous. In 1947, when doctors discovered that mercury was the cause of pink disease, the element was removed from teething powders and the disease became quite rare.

By the 1990s, after that Michigan family arrived at the doctor's office, the disease was not often seen in patients. It turned out that the family's home had recently been repainted. The house paint contained a chemical additive called phenylmercury(II) acetate ($C_8H_8HgO_2$). At the time, this form of mercury was not known to cause humans any harm. It was added to the paint to prevent the growth of mildew. Some of the mercury in the paint vaporized, or turned into a gas. This gas is colorless and odorless. The entire family breathed in some of the mercury vapor and suffered from varying degrees of mercury poisoning. Inhaled mercury vapor can be very dangerous.

Mercury is a cumulative poison, meaning that it builds up in the body over time. It is also a neurotoxin. Neurotoxins can destroy nerve tissue, including the brain. Chronic, or long-term, mercury exposure can lead to tremors (uncontrollable shaking or trembling), extreme mood changes, hearing loss, and blindness. These factors make exposure to even small amounts of mercury extremely dangerous. Mercury can enter the body through the skin, its vapor can be breathed in through the lungs, or it can enter through the digestive tract if food contaminated with mercury is eaten.

The saying "mad as a hatter" is also thought to have come from the use of a mercury compound, called mercury(II) nitrate, in the hat-making trade. This compound was used to make felt out of rabbit fur, and hats were manufactured with the felt. Workers in hat factories often suffered from serious health problems, such as the loss of

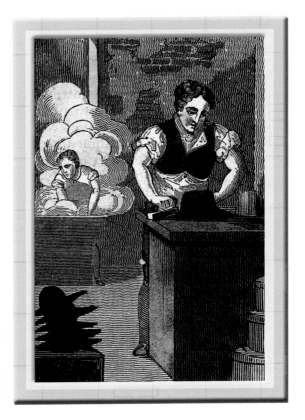

Workers in hat factories were often exposed to dangerous mercury vapors. Mercury, a neurotoxin, can build up in the body and destroy nervous tissue, including brain tissue.

teeth and hair, memory loss, and the deterioration of their nervous systems. This general breakdown of nervous tissue, especially in the brain, may have caused mental derangement and bizarre behavior, causing people to coin the term "mad as a hatter." Because of the health risk of mercury exposure, the U.S. Public Health Service banned the use of mercury(II) nitrate in the felt industry on December 1, 1941.

Chapter One
A Quick Look at Quicksilver

Mercury is the only metal that is a liquid at room temperature (68° Fahrenheit [20° Celsius]). Only one other element, the nonmetallic element bromine (Br), is a liquid under these conditions. Elements are substances that cannot be broken down into something simpler by using ordinary chemical means, such as exposing them to acids, electricity, or heat.

The History of Mercury

Mercury is a naturally occurring element in Earth's crust. It was known to the ancient Greeks, Romans, Chinese, and Hindus. Samples of the metal have been found in 3,500-year-old Egyptian tombs.

Mercury is a liquid at room temperature. Due to its appearance and how it moves, it's also called quicksilver.

Mercury was also a metal known to alchemists during the Middle Ages. The alchemists considered mercury, sulfur (S), and salt to be the three main substances that made up Earth. In fact, the Hindi word for alchemy, *rasasiddhi*, means "knowledge of mercury." Alchemists believed that all metals were mixtures of mercury and other substances. At the time, alchemists knew of seven metals: mercury, gold (Au), silver (Ag), copper (Cu), tin (Sn), lead (Pb), and iron (Fe). They also believed that, given the right combination of ingredients, mercury could be transmuted, or changed, into gold. Unfortunately for the alchemists, one element cannot be changed into another element through ordinary chemical means. So,

Because of its mobility, mercury was named for the Roman god Mercury *(center)*, the swift messenger of the gods. Alchemists believed mercury, sulfur, and salt were the three main substances that made up Earth.

no matter how hard they tried, they were unsuccessful at turning mercury, or any other metal, into gold.

Mercury's toxic effects were also known to the ancients. They could see the illnesses suffered by miners who dug mercury compounds from the ground. These ailments started with tremors and progressed to full-blown mental derangement, or madness.

Mercury's chemical symbol is Hg. The "Hg" comes from the Greek word *hydrargyrum.* *Hydrargyrum* means "liquid silver." Because of its silvery appearance and the way it moves, the metal was also called quicksilver. In fact, the element is named for the Roman god Mercury, who was known for his speed and mobility.

Where Is Mercury Found?

Mercury is rarely found in its pure state in nature. It occurs mostly in an ore called cinnabar. The scientific name for cinnabar is mercury(II) sulfide

(HgS). Cinnabar is a bright red mineral, sometimes called vermilion. Because of its bright red color, vermilion was a popular pigment, or coloring. About 20,000 years ago, ancient humans used cinnabar to make cave paintings. Scientists have also found prehistoric skulls painted with cinnabar in Italy. The

Archaeologists studied these cinnabar-covered remains in the ruins of Copan, Honduras. Ancient Mayans sometimes painted the remains of their dead with cinnabar, a bright red mineral of mercury.

A Mercury Fountain

Imagine filling a fountain with mercury instead of water. When the Spanish government approached Alexander Calder, an American sculptor and artist, to design a piece of art for the Spanish Pavilion at the 1937 World's Fair held in Paris, France, that is exactly what Calder did. Calder designed the fountain to remind people about the capture of the Almadén mercury mines by General Francisco Franco during the Spanish Civil War (1936–1939).

At the time of the capture, the Almadén mines supplied about 60 percent of the world's mercury. Today, Calder's mercury fountain can still be seen at the Fundación Joan Miró in Barcelona, Spain. To prevent people from inhaling mercury vapor, though, it is now displayed behind glass.

The mercury in Alexander Calder's mercury fountain continually recirculates. As the mercury runs down, it moves the red disk in the mobile.

pigment also has been discovered in Mayan ruins dating back to 500 BCE. Cinnabar is mainly found in Spain and Italy. Some mercury mines in Spain have been operating for more than 2,000 years.

Pure mercury can be gotten from cinnabar by heating the ore, in the presence of oxygen, to about 1100°F (590°C). The mercury in the rock turns to vapor, and the sulfur reacts with the oxygen to make sulfur dioxide. The mercury vapor is then cooled, causing it to condense into a liquid.

Sources of Mercury in the Environment

Traces of mercury are naturally found in many rocks and other substances, including coal. When coal that contains mercury is burned in power plants to make electricity, mercury is released into the atmosphere. Coal-burning power plants are responsible for more than 40 percent of the human-caused mercury emissions in the United States, making them the largest source. This mercury in the air eventually settles onto the waters of oceans, lakes, and streams, or onto land where it can be washed into the water and converted into dangerous mercury compounds by microorganisms.

Mercury and the Periodic Table

The periodic table is a chart that chemists use to organize the chemical elements based on the elements' properties. The rows on the periodic table are also called periods. Mercury is in period six. The columns on the periodic table are called groups or families. Mercury is found in group 12, or IIB (IIB is part of an old naming system), along with the elements zinc (Zn) and cadmium (Cd).

One of the first scientists to develop a periodic table was a Russian chemist named Dmitry Mendeleyev (also spelled Dmitri Mendeleev) (1834–1907). In Mendeleyev's time, only about sixty elements were known. He arranged these elements in a chart in order of their increasing atomic weights. When he did this, Mendeleyev saw that as long as he left a few blanks, the properties of the elements exhibited a periodic, or regular, pattern. Mendeleyev predicted that, one day, scientists would discover elements that had properties that would fill in the blanks in his chart. He even predicted what these properties would be. Eventually, Mendeleyev

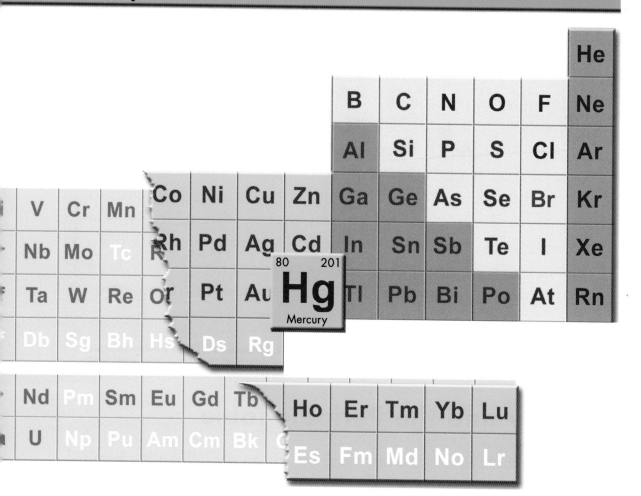

Mercury's chemical symbol is Hg, from the Greek word *hydrargyrum*. The element is located in period 6 and group 12 of the modern periodic table. Mercury is in the same group as zinc and cadmium, transition metals.

would be proven correct with the discoveries of gallium (Ga) in 1875, scandium (Sc) in 1879, and germanium (Ge) in 1886.

Elements can have two different types of properties—physical and chemical. Physical properties of mercury include that it is a shiny liquid at room temperature. The metal is heavy, too. In fact, if there were two identical cups, one that contained mercury and another that had the same volume of water in it, the cup with the mercury would weigh 13.6 times

Copper BBs will not sink through mercury (the bottom layer in this test tube) like they do through kerosene (the top layer) and water (the middle layer) because mercury is denser than copper.

more than the one containing the water. The property responsible for the difference in weight is called density. Because mercury is so dense, pieces of iron and lead will float on its surface. Another of mercury's physical properties is that the metal remains a liquid over a wide range of temperatures. Mercury freezes at −37.89°F (−38.83°C) and boils at 674.11°F (356.73°C).

Appearance, density, and melting and boiling temperatures are all physical properties. Mercury has chemical properties, too. Chemical properties describe how the element reacts with other chemicals that come into contact with it. For example, mercury will chemically combine with nonmetallic elements such as sulfur, oxygen (O), and chlorine (Cl) to make chemical compounds. Chemical compounds form when two or more elements are chemically bonded together.

Mercury is classified as a transition metal. Metals are substances that are shiny, conduct heat and electricity well, and are malleable and ductile when solid. Most of the elements on the periodic table are metals. Mercury has many of the properties of other metals, except it does not conduct heat very well. The transition metals are represented in groups 3 through 12 (or IIIB–IIB) on the periodic table (see pages 38–39).

Chapter Two
Mercury: The Inside Story

During Mendeleyev's time, only sixty elements were known, but today, scientists have discovered 111 elements, and several more are waiting to be verified. (See the periodic table of elements on pages 38–39.) Mendeleyev arranged his periodic table generally by the atomic weights of the elements. In 1913, however, Henry Moseley (1887–1915), a British physicist, discovered that an element's properties are determined more by its subatomic particles than by its weight.

Atomic Structure

Elements are made up of atoms. Atoms are the building blocks of all matter, which is anything that has mass and takes up space. A car, the air, and even you are all made up of atoms. An element is a substance that contains only one type of atom. A sample of pure mercury, for example, is made up of many, many tiny mercury atoms. Atoms contain three subatomic particles—protons, neutrons, and electrons.

All mercury atoms contain eighty protons. If an atom does not contain eighty protons, it is not an atom of mercury but an atom of some other element. An atom's atomic number is equal to its number of protons. Mercury's atomic number is eighty. The elements on the modern periodic table are listed in order of increasing atomic number. Arranged in this

All mercury atoms have 80 protons in their nucleus and 80 electrons traveling around the nucleus on six energy levels. On average, a mercury atom's nucleus also contains 121 neutrons.

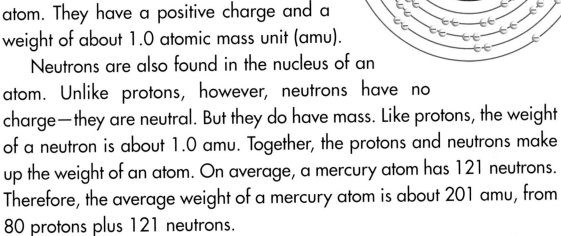

way, the elements in the same groups, or columns, have similar properties. Protons are located in the nucleus, or center, of the atom. They have a positive charge and a weight of about 1.0 atomic mass unit (amu).

Neutrons are also found in the nucleus of an atom. Unlike protons, however, neutrons have no charge—they are neutral. But they do have mass. Like protons, the weight of a neutron is about 1.0 amu. Together, the protons and neutrons make up the weight of an atom. On average, a mercury atom has 121 neutrons. Therefore, the average weight of a mercury atom is about 201 amu, from 80 protons plus 121 neutrons.

The third type of subatomic particle, the electron, has such a small mass that its weight is not used to calculate the weight of an atom. However, electrons are very important subatomic particles. Because protons, which are positively charged, and neutrons, which have no charge, make up the nucleus of an atom, the nucleus has a net positive charge. Nevertheless, atoms are neutral. That means that the positive charge in an atom's nucleus must be balanced by an equal number of negatively charged particles. These negatively charged subatomic particles are electrons. Because mercury atoms have eighty protons, they must also have eighty electrons.

The electrons travel around outside the nucleus and are arranged in shells, or energy levels. The electrons in the highest energy level, or outer-most shell, are called valence electrons. These valence electrons are lost, gained, or shared with other elements during chemical reactions. This exchange of electrons is what forms the chemical bonds between elements.

A chemical compound has properties that are different from either of the elements that make it up. Mercury(II) oxide (HgO), for example, is a yellow or red solid at room temperature.

When two or more elements are chemically bonded together, they form chemical compounds. For example, mercury has two valence electrons. When mercury chemically combines with oxygen, the mercury atom gives its two valance electrons to the oxygen atom. This creates a chemical bond between the mercury atom and the oxygen atom, and this results in a chemical compound called mercury(II) oxide (HgO).

Mercury Ions

When metals chemically react with nonmetals, the metal loses some or all of its valance electrons, and the nonmetallic element takes the electrons in. When a metal loses electrons, it has more protons in its nucleus than it has electrons. This gives the metal an overall positive charge. Because atoms are neutral, this charged particle is no longer called an atom. It is called an ion. The nonmetal atom that takes the electrons from mercury also forms an ion, a negative ion. The positive mercury ion and the negative nonmetal ion are attracted to each other by their opposite charges. This attraction forms a chemical bond, called an ionic bond because it involves ions.

Mercury is a transition metal. Transition metals often form more than one type of ion, and mercury is no exception. Sometimes, a mercury atom will lose both of its valance electrons. When this happens, the ion has two

Mercury Snapshot

Chemical Symbol:	Hg
Classification:	Transition metal
Properties:	Silvery white, mirrorlike liquid; high density
Discovered By:	Was known since ancient times
Atomic Number:	80
Atomic Weight:	200.59 atomic mass units (amu)
Protons:	80
Electrons:	80
Neutrons:	121 (on average)
State of matter at 68°F (20°C):	Liquid
Melting Point:	–37.89°F (–38.83°C)
Boiling Point:	674.11°F (356.73°C)
Commonly Found:	In Earth's crust, combined with the element sulfur in the mineral cinnabar (HgS) and the element chlorine in calomel (Hg_2Cl_2)

more protons than it has electrons. That means that this type of ion has a charge of +2. Another type of ion can be formed when a mercury atom loses only one of its two valence electrons. This results in an ion that has a charge of +1.

Because there are two forms of mercury ions, chemists developed a way to name mercury-containing chemical compounds that shows which type of ion is in the compound. To do this, they use a Roman numeral in the compound's name. The Roman numeral shows which type of ion is in the compound. When mercury combines with oxygen, for example, two different compounds can be formed: mercury(I) oxide (Hg_2O) and mercury(II) oxide (HgO). Mercury(I) oxide contains the ion that has a +1 charge. Mercury(II) oxide has the ion that has lost both valence electrons and has a charge of +2.

Isotopes of Mercury

Mercury's atomic weight is not always listed as exactly 201 amu on all periodic tables. That is because although all mercury atoms have the same

Alternate Names

There is an older way of naming the two different types of mercury ions. In this naming system, the +2 ion of mercury is called mercuric. The +1 mercury ion is called mercurous. Under this naming system, mercury(I) oxide would be named mercurous oxide, and the compound mercury(II) oxide would be called mercuric oxide. Most chemists today prefer to use the Roman numeral system, but the older naming system is still used on occasion.

number of protons, they do not all have the same number of neutrons. Forms of the same element that have different numbers of neutrons are called isotopes. The atomic weight listed on the periodic table takes into account all the different isotopes of mercury and in what proportion they are found.

There are seven naturally occurring isotopes of mercury. The most common mercury isotope is mercury-202. The number that appears after the element's name is its weight. Because all atoms of mercury have eighty protons, and the number of protons plus the number of neutrons adds up to an atom's weight, this isotope must have 122 neutrons. Almost 30 percent of all mercury atoms are mercury-202. The heaviest mercury isotope is

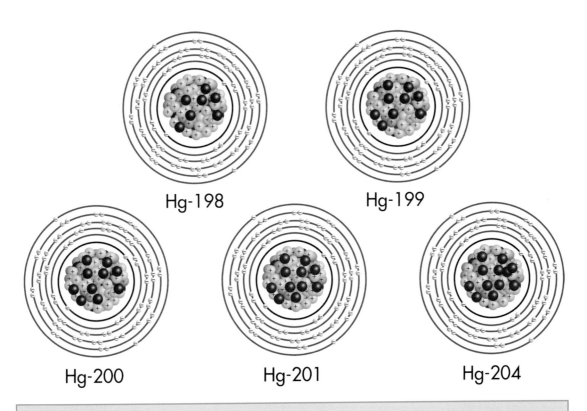

Hg-198   Hg-199

Hg-200   Hg-201   Hg-204

Isotopes have different weights because they have a different number of neutrons. An element's average atomic weight takes into account all of the element's isotopes and how often they occur.

mercury-204. Mercury-204 contains 124 neutrons and makes up about 7 percent of mercury atoms. The lightest and rarest mercury isotope is mercury-196. Less than 1 percent of all mercury atoms are mercury-196. The other four mercury isotopes are mercury-198, mercury-199, mercury-200, and mercury-201. Taking into account the masses and percents of the isotopes, the average weight of a mercury atom is 200.59 amu, the atomic weight that is listed on some periodic tables. This type of average is called a weighted average. On other periodic tables, such as the one in this book, mercury's atomic weight is rounded to the nearest whole number (201 amu).

Chapter Three
Elemental Mercury

If handled properly, mercury can be a very useful element. It is sometimes used in scientific instruments and household products such as thermometers, barometers, thermostats, silent wall switches, and fluorescent lightbulbs.

Thermometers

The first sealed, liquid-in-glass thermometer was invented by Ferdinand II (1610–1670), the Grand Duke of Tuscany, in 1654. His thermometer was filled with alcohol, but it was not very accurate. In 1714, Daniel Gabriel Fahrenheit (1686–1736), a German physicist, improved the

Ferdinand II de' Medici's alcohol thermometer consisted of small glass spheres of various densities that were submerged in vials containing alcohol.

accuracy of the thermometer by replacing the alcohol with mercury. New methods in glassblowing also helped improve the thermometer. Fahrenheit developed a standardized temperature scale that is still in use today, too.

Almost all liquids expand, or get bigger, when the temperature increases. The liquid inside a liquid-in-glass thermometer is held in a bulb at the bottom. The bulb is attached to a narrow tube at its top. When the liquid expands, there is nowhere for it to go but up into the tube, making the liquid move higher on the temperature scale. In addition, most liquids (with the notable exception of water) contract, or get smaller, when the temperature goes down. As the liquid contracts, it moves down the temperature scale, registering a lower temperature.

Mercury thermometers are still slightly more accurate than those filled with alcohol. If a mercury thermometer is broken, however, it can expose people to toxic mercury vapor. Because of these health concerns, many scientific laboratories and households are willing to sacrifice a little bit of accuracy in favor of safety. A red dye is often added to the alcohol to make it easier to see moving up and down the temperature scale.

In chemical laboratories, thermometers are not the only instruments that contain mercury, though. The element is also found in barometers (instruments that measure atmospheric pressure) and other scientific equipment. This

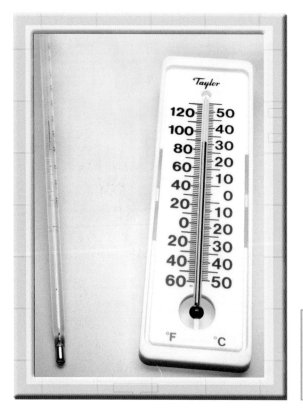

A mercury thermometer *(left)* is slightly more accurate than a modern alcohol thermometer *(right)*, but if the thermometer is broken, alcohol is safer.

How to Clean Up a Broken Mercury Thermometer

Follow these steps to clean up a broken mercury thermometer:

Ask everyone to leave the room. Make sure no one steps on the mercury. Remove pets, too. Open all windows and doors to the outside to help direct any mercury vapor outside and not into the rest of the house. Put on disposable latex, rubber, or nitrile gloves. Do not touch the mercury without gloves. Carefully pick up any broken glass. Wrap the glass in a paper towel and put it in a zip-top bag.

If the mercury spill is on a hard, smooth surface, use a piece of cardboard or a squeegee to collect any mercury beads that can be seen. Once the mercury is all in one place, use an eyedropper to suck up the mercury. When the eyedropper is full, squeeze the mercury onto a wet paper towel and put it in a zip-top bag.

Go around the area with duct tape to collect the harder-to-see mercury beads, using the tape as if you were trying to get lint off of your clothes. Put the tape in a zip-top bag, too.

If the mercury spills on carpet, curtains, or other absorbent material, cut away the part that is contaminated and place it in a trash bag.

Put all of the zip-top bags, gloves, cardboard, and any other items used during the cleanup in a heavy-duty trash bag. (Triple bagging, using three zip-top bags—one inside the other—and placing them inside a wide-mouth plastic container, is recommended.) Take the bag to your community's hazardous waste collection center. Call your local health department to inquire about air-quality testing before resuming use of the room. Never throw mercury in the trash.

can pose a health risk to chemists working in laboratories where these instruments are found. If a thermometer, barometer, or other piece of equipment is broken, for example, the mercury can fill cracks on lab benches and floors and be very hard to clean up. Mercury that is not properly disposed of can easily vaporize, endangering the safety of laboratory workers.

Mercury Switches

Mercury, like most other metals, conducts electricity. Because of this property, mercury has been used in electrical switches and thermostats. Mercury light switches look just like regular ones, but they do not "click" like other types of light switches do when you flip them. For this reason, these switches are sometimes called silent switches. Mercury light switches were made and sold from the late 1960s to 1991. They can still be found in some older homes and businesses. When the light switch is flipped on, the mercury moves to surround electrical contacts inside the switch. This action completes an electrical circuit that allows electricity to flow through wires and turn the light on. When the light switch is turned off, the mercury moves away from the electrical contacts. This movement breaks the circuit and turns the light out.

A thermostat is the device that monitors and controls when the heat or air-conditioner comes on or goes off. Many thermostats contain mercury tilt switches. The mercury in these switches is enclosed in a small glass capsule. Inside the capsule, there are electrical contacts at one end. When the switch is tilted, the mercury collects at the end with the contacts, where it completes a circuit that allows electricity to flow through. When the mercury goes to the other end, the circuit is broken.

As long as the silent wall switches and thermostats are in good working condition, there is no health risk from the mercury switches inside these devices. However, if they are removed, they should be taken to a household hazardous waste collection center, not tossed into the trash.

Inside a mercury tilt switch, liquid mercury surrounds electrical contacts. When a tilt switch is used in a thermostat, such as the one pictured here, this completes an electrical circuit and turns the heating unit on.

Fluorescent Lights

Mercury is found not only in light switches but also in some lightbulbs. The long glass bulb of a fluorescent light is filled with a small amount of mercury vapor and argon (Ar) gas. When electricity is passed through the bulb, electrons in the mercury atoms absorb enough energy to move them to a higher energy level. This is called the excited state. When the electrons fall back to their regular energy level, their ground state, they give off radiation, some of which is ultraviolet (UV). However, humans cannot see UV radiation. To convert UV radiation to visible light, the insides of fluorescent lightbulbs are coated with a chemical powder called a phosphor. When the phosphor is hit by UV radiation, the phosphor's electrons are excited to a higher energy level, too. When those electrons fall back to their ground state, they emit visible light.

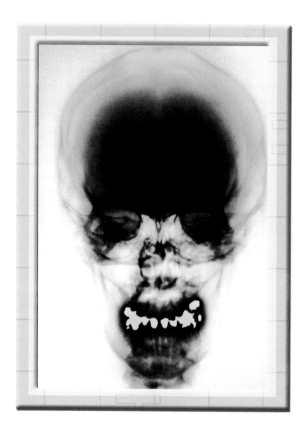

Silver-colored dental fillings, used to fill cavities, are made of an amalgam, or mixture, of mercury and silver. The fillings show up on a dental X-ray.

Amalgams

One unusual characteristic of mercury is that it will dissolve other metals. When other metals are dissolved in mercury, they form a special type of alloy called an amalgam. Alloys are mixtures of two or more elements, at least one of which is a metal. Alloys are used because their properties are different from those of the elements they are made up of. Mercury alloys are called amalgams. Amalgams can be liquid or solid.

Dental amalgams are used by dentists to make fillings for cavities. They are made by dissolving silver dust in mercury. When a silver-mercury dental amalgam is first mixed, it is a liquid. However, it hardens quickly. As it hardens, the amalgam expands to fill the hole where the cavity formed in the tooth.

Gold will also dissolve in mercury. As a result, mercury is often used to extract gold from its ore. The gold-mercury amalgam is then heated. The mercury turns into a vapor, and pure gold is left behind. When the mercury vapor is cooled, it condenses back into a liquid, and it can be used again.

Chapter Four
Mercury Compounds

Mercury is not used only in its pure form, though. Chemical compounds that contain mercury can also be quite useful at times. Chemical compounds are formed when two or more elements are chemically bonded together.

But mercury and its compounds can be very toxic, too. Some metals, such as sodium (Na), iron, and zinc, are essential for the human body to work properly. Unlike these metals, mercury has no biological purpose in the human body. Once inside the body, mercury can chemically react with enzymes. Enzymes are proteins that are essential for the body to function properly. When mercury reacts with the body's enzymes, the enzymes are chemically changed, and they can no longer do the job that they normally do.

Poisons

The same properties that make mercury poisonous to humans also make the metal poisonous to insects, fungi, and bacteria. Mercury(II) chloride ($HgCl_2$), for example, is a very poisonous salt. It is also soluble, which means that it can be dissolved in water. It was once used as a fungicide, a chemical substance that destroys fungus, and as a pesticide, a chemical substance that kills rodents, such as rats. In the past, it also has been

MERCVRE.

A woodcut from 1657 shows the medicinal use of mercury. Despite mercury's toxic nature, mercury compounds were used in the past as medicines to soothe sore gums and to treat digestive problems and sexually transmitted diseases.

used to keep wood from rotting, as well as to disinfect surfaces and wounds. Because the compound is so poisonous, though, scientists have tried to find other chemicals to take the place of mercury(II) chloride. Some small, buttonlike batteries that power watches, calculators, and toys, however, still contain the compound today.

Mercury(II) chloride is not the only poisonous salt of mercury. Mercury(I) chloride (Hg_2Cl_2) is toxic, too. But mercury(I) chloride does not dissolve in water as easily as mercury(II) chloride does, so it is not as dangerous. Mercury(I) chloride is also called calomel. Calomel was once used as an antiseptic. Antiseptics slow the growth of bacteria. Doctors formerly prescribed the compound as an internal medicine, too. It was given because it serves as a strong laxative, and it was used to treat syphilis, a sexually transmitted disease. Calomel was also a common ingredient in teething powders, which were used to soothe the sore gums of babies cutting new teeth, until the dangers of the compound were discovered and publicized in 1948. Today, calomel is sometimes employed in agriculture to control root maggots and other pests on underground plant parts, such as tubers, roots, and bulbs.

Kaboom!

Another mercury compound, mercury(II) fulminate [$Hg(ONC)_2$], is dangerous in another way. It is highly explosive and used to make blasting caps. The explosive is very sensitive to friction (rubbing) and shock (striking). In fact, the compound is so sensitive that accidents are common and much care needs to be taken when dealing with this explosive.

Mercury Batteries

Mercury(II) chloride is not the only mercury compound that has been used in batteries. Mercury(II) oxide (HgO) was once used as the positive electrode, or cathode, in dry cell batteries such as the ones found in radios, flashlights, and portable CD players. The negative electrode, or the anode, of these batteries is usually made of zinc. The advantage of a mercury battery over other batteries is that it can supply a constant voltage, even when it gets old and the

Alkaline batteries (AA, AAA, and C batteries, for example) once contained mercury, but now other chemicals are used in these batteries instead. Many button batteries, however, still contain mercury.

battery is partially drained. The disadvantage is that its mercury is highly toxic and needs to be properly disposed of. Because many people did not take proper care and just tossed these batteries in their household trash, however, mercury batteries have been banned in the United States since the 1980s. Nevertheless, a report released in 1994, fourteen years after the ban, revealed that almost 88 percent of the total mercury found in landfills still came from mercury batteries. Mercury batteries are even now sold in some parts of Europe and Asia.

Eating fish contaminated with methylmercury can cause nerve and brain damage. Unborn babies and small children are especially vulnerable to the effects of mercury poisoning.

Organic Compounds

All of the mercury compounds discussed previously are inorganic compounds. Inorganic compounds are compounds that are not derived from living organisms. Scientists have found, however, that some microorganisms (microscopic organisms that are too small to be seen with the human eye) can convert mercury into an organic compound. Organic compounds are compounds that contain the element carbon (C). They often have the elements hydrogen (H) and oxygen in them, too. The microorganisms that the scientists found live in lakes, streams, and rivers. When it rains, mercury-containing compounds run off of the land and into the water. Additional mercury enters the water through the emissions of coal-burning power plants and waste incinerators (places where trash is burned). Once the mercury is in the water, the microorganisms absorb the mercury. Then they chemically change the mercury into an organic compound called methylmercury.

Small fish eat the microorganisms that contain the methylmercury and the compound builds up in the fish's tissues. Larger fish eat the smaller fish and more and more mercury accumulates in the food chain. This accumulation is called biomagnification. Humans, who eventually eat the larger fish, get a fairly high dose of methylmercury from them. Unfortunately, the organic form of mercury is much more dangerous to humans than the inorganic mercury. When inside the human body, methylmercury can cause neurological and brain damage. In pregnant women, too much methylmercury can also lead to birth defects in the baby. Because of the risk of mercury poisoning, efforts by governments and scientists are being made to reduce the amount of mercury-containing substances that find their way into the water supply.

Chapter Five
Mercury Poisoning

Mercury can enter the body through the lungs, the digestive tract, or the skin. However, the amount of mercury that will be absorbed depends on how the element gets into the body. For example, because the lungs are very efficient at absorbing mercury vapor, the vapor is much more dangerous to humans than liquid mercury.

Soluble mercury compounds are also quite dangerous because they are easily absorbed by the body. Small amounts of mercury can be eliminated by the body without doing much harm because the kidneys produce a protein that can bind very tightly with mercury atoms. Consequently, limited exposure to small amounts of metallic mercury and insoluble mercury compounds does not have the same effect on the body as exposure to vaporized mercury, soluble mercury compounds, and organic mercury compounds.

Mercury in Fish

Officials at the U.S. Environmental Protection Agency (EPA) and the Food and Drug Administration (FDA) are very concerned about the possible health effects caused by eating fish contaminated with methylmercury. For this reason, the EPA and the FDA work together to provide the public with guidelines about which species of fish should be avoided.

A mother bathes her daughter, who has physical disabilities stemming from the mercury-contaminated waters of Minamata Bay, Japan. In the late 1950s, industrial pollution surrounding the bay contaminated the waters with mercury.

The first documented example of methylmercury poisoning occurred in Japan in 1958. Fishermen and their families who lived in the area around Minamata Bay on the Japanese island of Kyushu started to get sick. In the end, sixty-eight people died and almost four hundred others exhibited some level of neurological damage. Scientists later found that local industries were discharging elemental mercury into the bay. Bacteria living in the water turned the metallic mercury into methylmercury. The fishermen and their families got so sick because they ate a lot of fish that they caught in the bay.

Methylmercury affects the central nervous system and can cause paralysis, "tunnel vision," and blindness. It is also very dangerous to unborn babies. A baby exposed to methylmercury in the womb may be born with

Science Matters

These predatory fish shown at right, when full-grown, contain so much mercury that health officials advise that they not be eaten

King mackerel

Swordfish

Scalloped hammerhead shark

Tilefish

How fish become toxic

Some saltwater and freshwater fish are contaminated with mercury, a toxic heavy metal, because of what they eat.

What is a food chain?

Each plant and animal species in a natural community eats some species and is eaten by others

Biologists call this web of relationships a food chain

Black bass

Sunfish

Scavengers eat dead fish, develop high mercury levels

Crayfish

Minnows

Higher-level predators eat smaller predator fish; bodies may contain high levels of mercury

Lower-level predators eat fish, other animals; mercury collects in their bodies

Plant-eaters bring mercury into food chain; contain low amounts of mercury

People most at risk

☐ **Pregnant women** and women who may become pregnant
☐ **Nursing mothers**
☐ **Children up to age 10**

Mercury can seriously damage the fast-growing brain and nervous system of a child or fetus

Lifespan matters: Predators and scavengers that live for several years have longer time to concentrate mercury than fish that die relatively young

Path of mercury pollution

1 Coal- and oil-burning power plants and waste incinerators send mercury into air

2 Water bacteria turn mercury into toxic methyl mercury

3 Small aquatic plants and animals store methyl mercury

4 Toxin gradually works its way up food chain to larger fish, which humans eat

© 2003 KRT

Safer food choices

More than once a week: Salmon, shrimp, farm-raised catfish and rainbow trout, flounder, sole, perch, tilapia, clams, scallops

No more than once a week: Tuna (canned), crab, cod, mahi-mahi, herring, haddock, whitefish

Source: U.S. Food and Drug Admin., U.S. Environmental Protection Agency, Florida Sportsman, Florida Fish & Wildlife Conservation Commission, KRT Illustration Bank
Graphic: Cindy Jones-Hulfachor, Sun Sentinel

neurological damage that resembles cerebral palsy, if it survives at all. (Cerebral palsy is a disability resulting from damage to the brain at or before birth that can cause muscular incoordination and speech problems.) For this reason, the EPA and FDA recommend that pregnant women avoid fish that may be contaminated with methylmercury.

Yet, eating fish can be an important part of a healthy diet. For example, scientific studies have shown that eating fish can lead to a lower likelihood of developing heart disease. Fish are low in fat and high in protein and omega-3 fatty acids. The trick is to eat enough heart-healthy fish without being exposed to too much mercury. For most people, the risk of eating fish or shellfish contaminated with mercury is not much of a health concern. In spite of this, for some people, such as women who are pregnant or hoping to get pregnant, nursing mothers, and young children, fish with high levels of methylmercury should be avoided.

The amount of methylmercury that builds up in fish depends on what type of fish it is, what it eats, and how high on the food chain it is. For example, large fish at the top of the food chain, such as shark, swordfish, or king mackerel, are much more likely to contain high levels of methylmercury. Therefore, shrimp, salmon, pollock, and catfish are better choices for pregnant women and young children because they contain lower methylmercury levels. The FDA and the EPA recommend eating up to 12 ounces, or two average meals, that contain these fish per week.

Mercury Poisoning

Eating fish is not the only way that people can be exposed to mercury. For example, in 1971–1972, more than 6,500 Iraqis fell ill and almost

Large fish at the top of the food chain are more likely to contain higher levels of methylmercury. Health officials advise people against eating large fish, such as swordfish and king mackerel.

500 died when several countries responded to a famine by shipping to Iraq wheat intended for planting. Unfortunately, the wheat grains had been treated with a fungicide to keep mold from growing on the grain. The fungicide contained methylmercury. The seeds were colored with a red dye to warn people of the danger of eating the seeds directly. But the warnings on the seed bags were not printed in a language understood by the Iraqis. So, many Iraqi families ground the red-dyed wheat grains into flour. They used this flour to make bread. When they ate the bread baked with the contaminated flour, they became ill. The use of methylmercury as a fungicide is now banned in the United States. Because fungicide was the only commercial use for the compound, it is no longer made.

People are rarely in danger of mercury poisoning from using mercury thermometers in their homes. However, in the 1970s and 1980s, workers at a mercury thermometer plant in Vermont began to notice a common set of heath problems. When the workers were tested, mercury was found in

their bodies. Mercury vapor was also found in the air in the workers' homes, on their clothing and furniture, and in their children's bodies. This incident was the first time that children of people who worked with mercury were known to be affected by their parents' exposure to the element. The plant closed in 1984.

Karen Wetterhahn, a Dartmouth chemistry professor, was poisoned by a rare form of mercury she was working with. Dimethylmercury seeped through her glove and into her skin. She died in ten months.

Mercury in Vaccines

Thimerosal, a mercury-containing preservative, has been used in vaccines since the 1930s. Other than minor reactions, such as redness and swelling at the site of the shot, scientists have not discovered any side effects due to the mercury. In 1999, however, the American Academy of Pediatrics and the Public Health Service recommended that thimerosal in vaccines be reduced or eliminated, just in case. Today, with the exception of some flu shots, none of the childhood vaccines administered in the United States contain thimerosal.

In 1997, a Dartmouth College chemistry professor, Dr. Karen Wetterhahn, tragically died of mercury poisoning at the age of forty-eight. A toxic metals specialist, Wetterhahn was unintentionally poisoned when a few drops of a deadly compound of mercury, called dimethylmercury, got on the protective glove she was wearing. Unfortunately, later tests showed that dimethylmercury can seep through the type of glove that Wetterhahn was wearing. Six months later, she started to show symptoms of mercury poisoning, but, by that time, there was nothing that could be done to reverse the damage done by the mercury compound. She died a little less than a year after her accidental exposure to dimethylmercury. Now, scientists know that the only safe way to handle dimethylmercury is by wearing a special, heavy-duty type of glove.

Because of the risk of mercury poisoning, and that mercury is an element and thus cannot be broken down, people must be very careful how they handle and dispose of objects that contain mercury. Always make sure that mercury batteries, thermometers, and fluorescent lightbulbs are taken to a hazardous waste disposal site and not just thrown in your household trash. Taking these precautionary measures will keep as much mercury as possible out of landfills, water supplies, and your body.

The Periodic Table of Elements

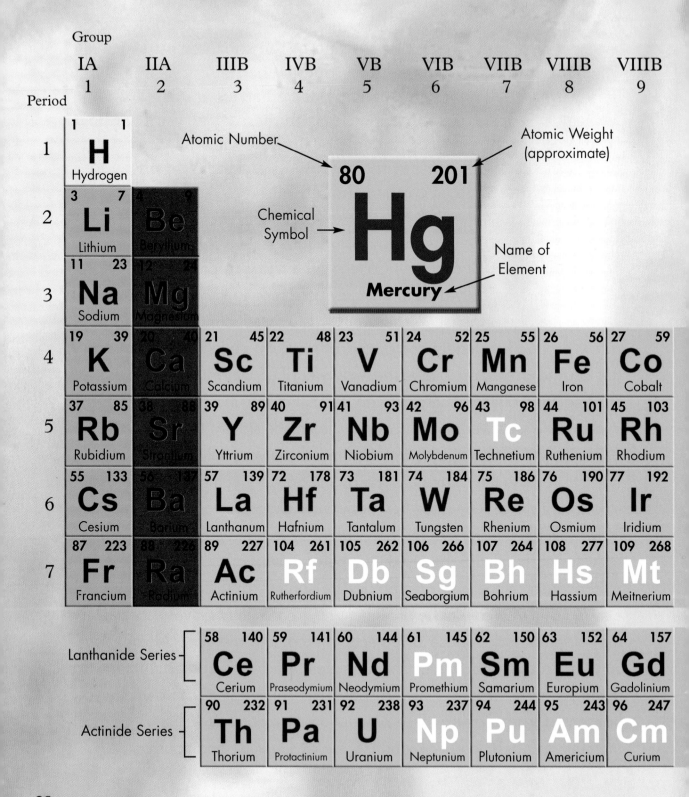

Group

| IA | IIA | IIIB | IVB | VB | VIB | VIIB | VIIIB | VIIIB |
| 1 | 2 | 3 | 4 | 5 | 6 | 7 | 8 | 9 |

Period

Atomic Number

Atomic Weight (approximate)

80	201
Hg	
Mercury	

Chemical Symbol

Name of Element

Period 1								
1 1 **H** Hydrogen								
3 7 **Li** Lithium	4 9 **Be** Beryllium							
11 23 **Na** Sodium	12 24 **Mg** Magnesium							
19 39 **K** Potassium	20 40 **Ca** Calcium	21 45 **Sc** Scandium	22 48 **Ti** Titanium	23 51 **V** Vanadium	24 52 **Cr** Chromium	25 55 **Mn** Manganese	26 56 **Fe** Iron	27 59 **Co** Cobalt
37 85 **Rb** Rubidium	38 88 **Sr** Strontium	39 89 **Y** Yttrium	40 91 **Zr** Zirconium	41 93 **Nb** Niobium	42 96 **Mo** Molybdenum	43 98 **Tc** Technetium	44 101 **Ru** Ruthenium	45 103 **Rh** Rhodium
55 133 **Cs** Cesium	56 137 **Ba** Barium	57 139 **La** Lanthanum	72 178 **Hf** Hafnium	73 181 **Ta** Tantalum	74 184 **W** Tungsten	75 186 **Re** Rhenium	76 190 **Os** Osmium	77 192 **Ir** Iridium
87 223 **Fr** Francium	88 226 **Ra** Radium	89 227 **Ac** Actinium	104 261 **Rf** Rutherfordium	105 262 **Db** Dubnium	106 266 **Sg** Seaborgium	107 264 **Bh** Bohrium	108 277 **Hs** Hassium	109 268 **Mt** Meitnerium

Lanthanide Series

| 58 140 **Ce** Cerium | 59 141 **Pr** Praseodymium | 60 144 **Nd** Neodymium | 61 145 **Pm** Promethium | 62 150 **Sm** Samarium | 63 152 **Eu** Europium | 64 157 **Gd** Gadolinium |

Actinide Series

| 90 232 **Th** Thorium | 91 231 **Pa** Protactinium | 92 238 **U** Uranium | 93 237 **Np** Neptunium | 94 244 **Pu** Plutonium | 95 243 **Am** Americium | 96 247 **Cm** Curium |

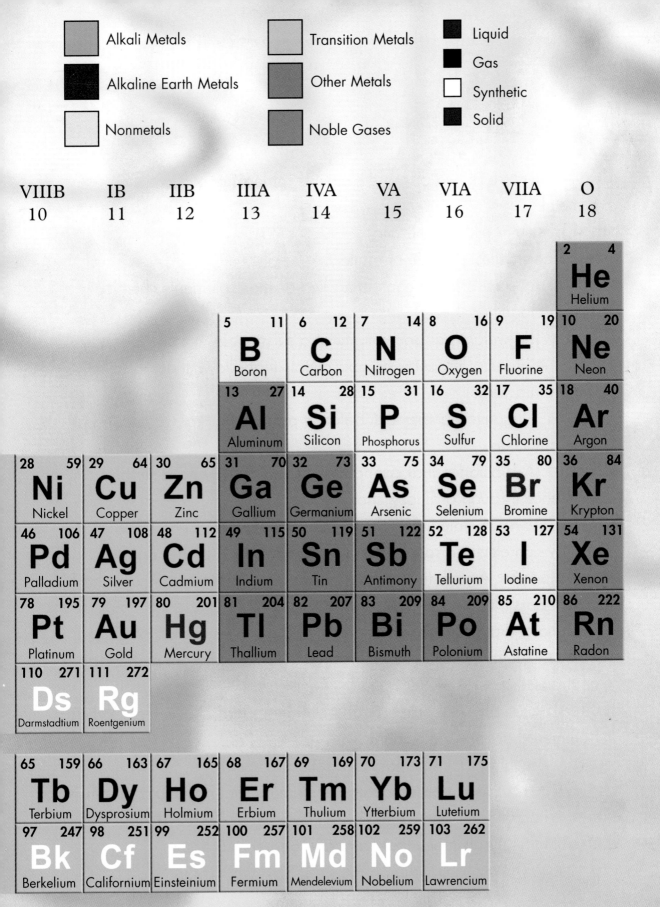

Glossary

alloy A mixture of two or more elements, at least one of which is a metal.

amalgam An alloy of mercury.

atom The smallest particle of matter.

compound A substance containing two or more elements chemically bonded together.

density The weight per unit volume of a substance.

ductile A physical property of most metals that allows them to be drawn into wires.

electron Negatively charged subatomic particle that moves around an atom's nucleus.

element A substance that cannot be broken down into a simpler substance through ordinary chemical means.

excited state A state in which an atom has absorbed enough energy to move an electron from a lower energy level to a higher one.

ground state A state in which all of an atom's electrons occupy the lowest possible energy levels.

ion A charged particle formed when valence electrons are lost or gained.

isotopes Atoms of the same element that have a different number of neutrons.

malleable A physical property of most metals that allows them to be hammered or rolled into sheets.

matter Anything that has mass and takes up space.

methylmercury An organic form of mercury that accumulates in fish as they grow older and larger.

neurotoxin A substance that can damage nervous tissue.

neutron A neutral subatomic particle found in the nucleus of an atom.

nucleus The tiny center of an atom, which contains nearly all of its mass.

organic compound A chemical compound that contains carbon and is derived from a living (or once living) organism.

proton A positively charged subatomic particle that is found in the nucleus of an atom.

transition metals Metals that are found in groups 3 through 12 (or IIIB–IB) on the periodic table.

valance electrons Electrons in an atom's outermost shell, in the highest energy level.

Environment Canada
Inquiry Center
70 Crémazie Street
Gatineau, QC
Canada
K1A 0H3
(800) 668-6767 (in Canada only) or (819) 997-2800
Web site: http://www.ec.gc.ca
Environment Canada's Web site provides pdf documents about mercury
    pollution and mercury reduction programs.

National Electrical Manufacturers Association (NEMA)
1300 North 17th Street, Suite 1752
Rosslyn, VA 22209
(703) 841-3200
Web site: http://www.nema.org
NEMA provides information on how to safely dispose of and recycle
    mercury-containing fluorescent lightbulbs.

National Institute of Environmental Health Sciences (NIEHS)
P.O. Box 12233
Research Triangle Park, NC 27709
(919) 541-0395
Web site: http://www.niehs.nih.gov
NIEHS's Web site explains environmental health topics, such as symptoms
    of heavy metal exposure.

Northeast Waste Management Officials' Association (NEWMOA)
Interstate Mercury Education & Reduction Clearinghouse (IMERC)
129 Portland Street, 6th Floor
Boston, MA 02114
(617) 367-8558 x307
Web site: http://www.newmoa.org
NEWMOA's mercury reduction program, IMERC, maintains a database
    to inform consumers about products containing mercury and the
    amount of mercury in them.

U.S. Environmental Protection Agency (EPA)
Ariel Rios Building
1200 Pennsylvania Avenue NW
Washington, DC 20460
(202) 272-0167
Web site: http://www.epa.gov
If you are looking for which fish are safe to eat, the EPA provides fish
    advisories for each state and body of water. An interactive map on
    the EPA's Superfund Web site also can help you find toxic waste sites
    near where you live.

Web Sites

Due to the changing nature of Internet links, Rosen Publishing has
developed an online list of Web sites related to the subject of this book.
This site is updated regularly. Please use this link to access the list:

http://www.rosenlinks.com/uept/merc

Barber, Ian. *Sorting the Elements: The Periodic Table at Work*. Vero Beach, FL: Rourke Publishing, 2008.

Kirkland, Kyle. *Atoms and Materials*. New York, NY: Facts on File, Inc., 2007.

Manning, Phillip. *Atoms, Molecules, and Compounds*. New York, NY: Chelsea House Publications, 2007.

Miller, Ron. *The Elements. What You Really Want to Know*. Minneapolis, MN: Lerner Publishing Group, 2004.

Newton, David. *Chemistry of the Environment*. New York, NY: Facts on File, Inc., 2007.

Parks, Peggy J. *Toxic Waste* (Our Environment). San Diego, CA: KidHaven Press, 2006.

Watt, Susan. *The Elements: Mercury*. New York, NY: Benchmark Books, 2004.

White, Katherine. *Mendeleyev and the Periodic Table*. New York, NY: Rosen Publishing Group, 2005.

Bibliography

Blanc, Paul. *How Everyday Products Make People Sick: Toxins at Home and in the Workplace.* Berkeley, CA: University of California Press, 2007.

Center for Environmental Health Sciences at Dartmouth. "Mercury: Element of the Ancients." March 30, 2005. Retrieved October 11, 2007 (http://www.dartmouth.edu/~toxmetal/TXSHhg.shtml).

Centers for Disease Control and Prevention. "Mercury and Vaccines (Thimerosal)." June 5, 2007. Retrieved October 11, 2007 (http://www.cdc.gov/od/science/iso/concerns/thimerosal.htm).

City of St. Louis Refuse Division. "Household Batteries: Reduction, Reuse, and Recycling." Retrieved October 11, 2007 (http://stlouis.missouri.org/citygov/recycle/batteries.html).

Cobb, Cathy, and Harold Goldwhite. *Creations of Fire: Chemistry's Lively History from Alchemy to the Atomic Age.* New York, NY: Plenum Press, 1995.

Jefferson Lab. "It's Elemental—the Element Mercury." Retrieved October 11, 2007 (http://education.jlab.org/itselemental/ele080.html).

New Hampshire Department of Environmental Services. "Cleaning Up Household Spills of Elemental Mercury (Hg)." Retrieved October 11, 2007 (http://www.des.state.nh.us/factsheets/hw/hw-15.htm).

The Ordnance Shop. "Mercury Fulminate." Retrieved October 11, 2007 (http://www.ordnance.org/mercury.htm).

S. Brannan and Sons, Ltd. "Who Invented the Thermometer?" Retrieved October 11, 2007 (http://www.brannan.co.uk/thermometers/invention.html).

Stwertka, Albert. *A Guide to the Elements.* 2nd ed. New York, NY: Oxford University Press, 2002.

University of California–Berkeley. "Mercury." Retrieved October 11, 2007 (http://socrates.berkeley.edu/~eps2/wisc/hg.html).

U.S. Environmental Protection Agency. "Mercury." August 7, 2007. Retrieved October 10, 2007 (http://www.epa.gov/mercury/about.htm).

U.S. Environmental Protection Agency. "What You Need to Know About Mercury in Fish and Shellfish." July 19, 2007. Retrieved October 11, 2007 (http://www.epa.gov/waterscience/fishadvice/advice.html).

About the Author

Kristi Lew is a professional K–12 educational writer with degrees in biochemistry and genetics. A former high school science teacher, she specializes in writing textbooks, magazine articles, and nonfiction books about science, health, and the environment for students and teachers.

Photo Credits

Cover, pp. 1, 12, 38–39 Tahara Anderson; p. 5 © Ann Ronan Picture Library/Heritage-Images/The Image Works; p. 7 © Dirk Wiersma/Photo Researchers, Inc.; p. 8 © Charles Walker/Topfoto/The Image Works; p. 9 © Kenneth Garrett/National Geographic/Getty Images; pp. 10, 16 Wikipedia; pp. 13, 22, 25 © Charles D. Winters/Photo Researchers, Inc.; p. 21 © Tomsich/Photo Researchers, Inc.; p. 26 © Scott Camazine/Science Photo Library/Photo Researchers, Inc.; p. 28 © SSPL/The Image Works; p. 29 © www.istockphoto.com/Bernd Neisemann; p. 30 © Charles Philip Cangialosi/Corbis; p. 33 © W. Eugene Smith (1918–78)/Israel Museum, Jerusalem, Israel, Gift of Mr. and Mrs. Dan Berley, New York/The Bridgeman Art Library; p. 34 © Jones-Hulfachor/Sun Sentinel/Newscom; p. 36 © AP Images.

Designer: Tahara Anderson; **Editor:** Kathy Kuhtz Campbell
Photo Researcher: Amy Feinberg